My Little Advent Christmas Coloring Book

December 1

Ideas for using this book:

*Color one picture or do an activity every day during Advent. Use crayons,markers, or colored pencils.

Angel

December 2

Mary and Baby Jesus

December 3

Joseph and Baby Jesus

December 4

Camel
Sheep

December 5

Baby Jesus

December 6

Wise Man and gift

December 7

Angel and gifts

December 8

Wise Men Crowns

December 9

Manger

December 10

Donkey
Ox

December 11

Wise Man and gift

December 12

Use the grid to draw the star.

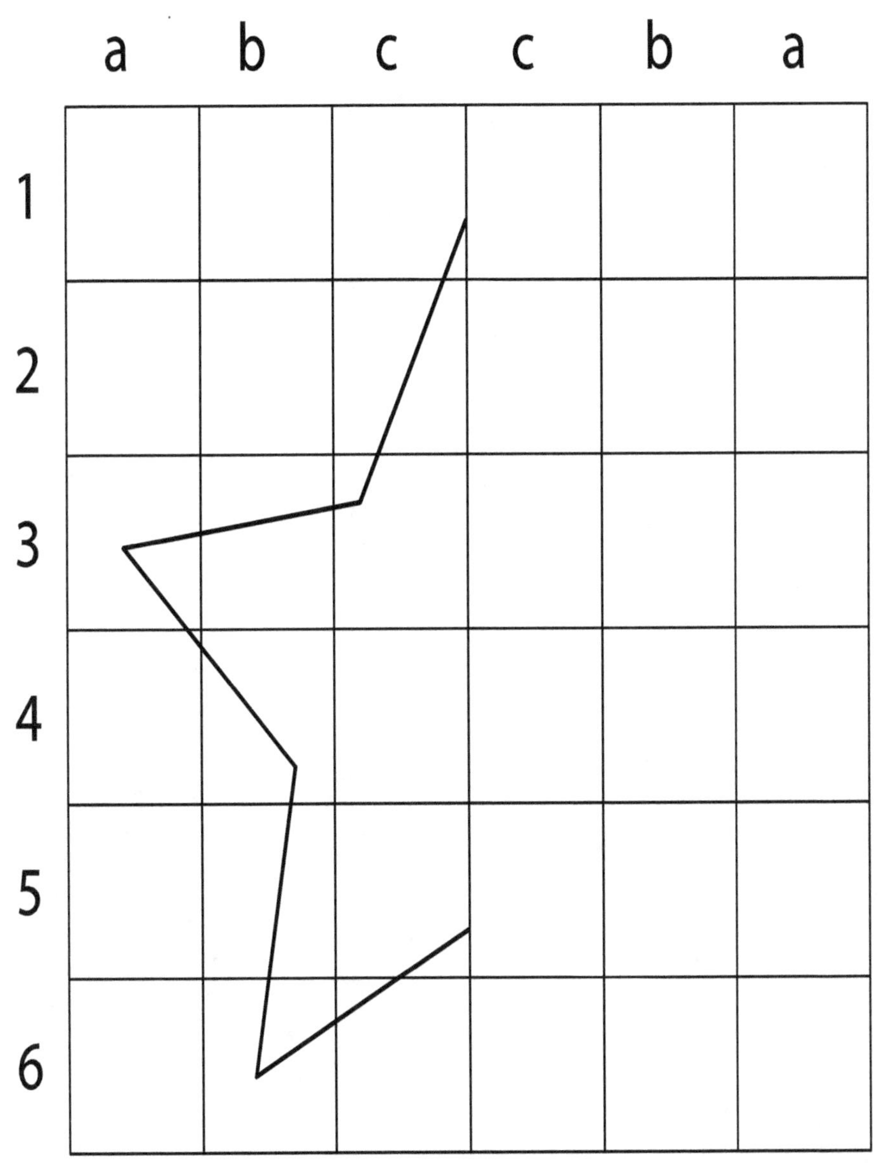

December 13

Connect the dots and color the boy singing a Christmas carol.

December 14

Christmas stocking

December 15

Decorate the Christmas tree and gifts.

December 16

Angel

December 17

Reindeer

December 18

Connect the dots and color the girl singing a Christmas carol.

December 19

Learn how to draw an angel.

December 20

Connect the dots and color the bell.

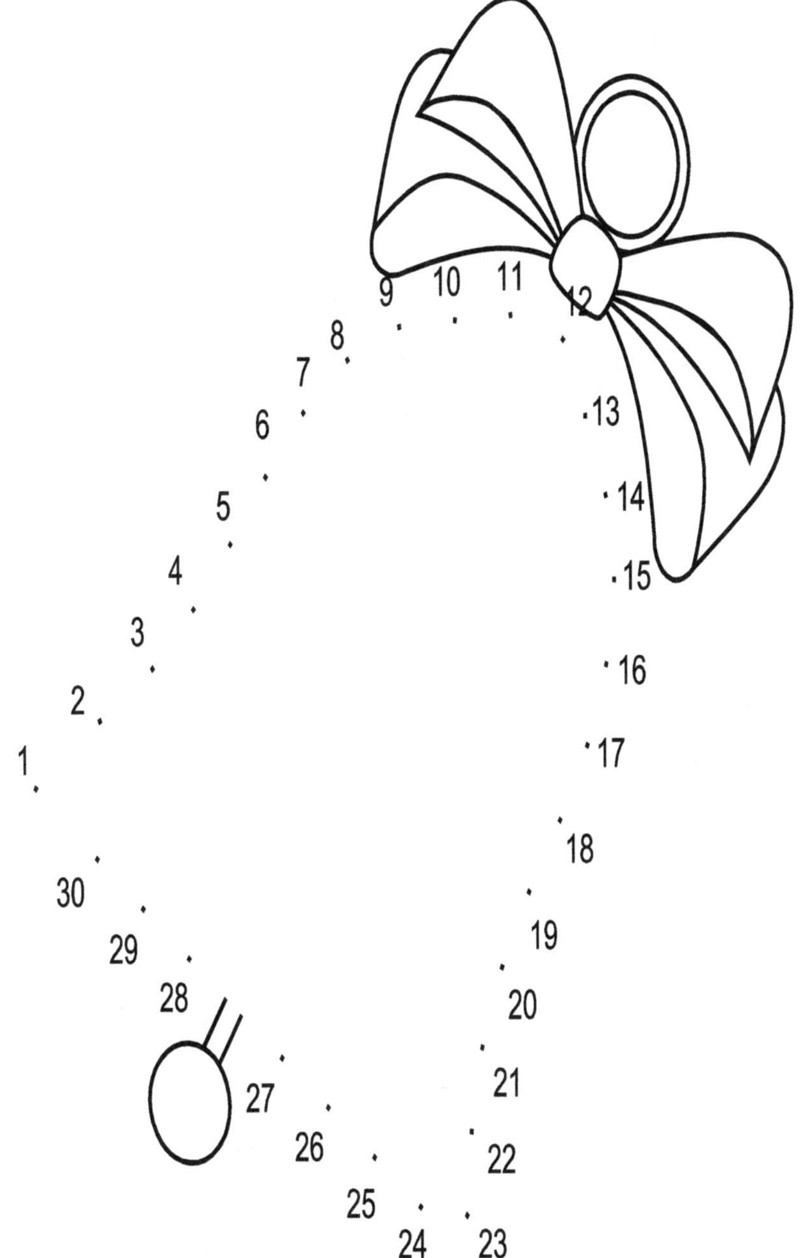

December 21

Fireplace with stockings

December 22

Christmas candle

December 23

Use the grid to draw the gift.

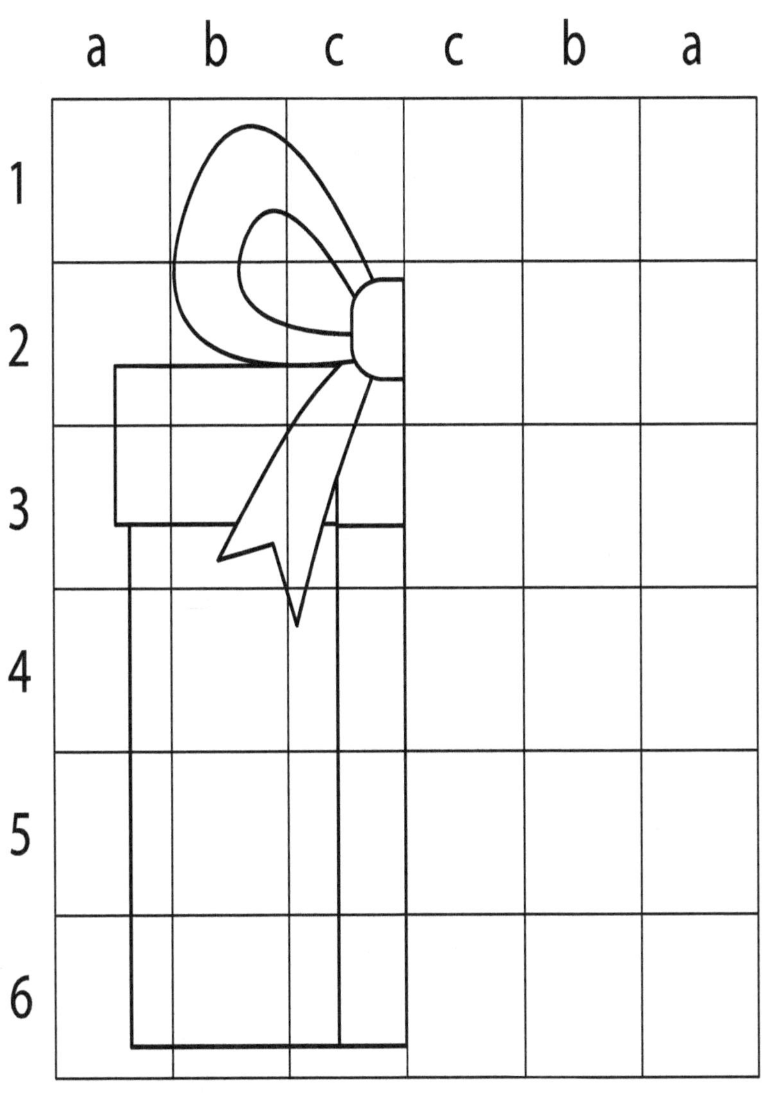

December 24

Angels praying over Baby Jesus.

December 25

Decorate the Christmas Cake!

From,

____

florabellapublishing.com